God's
GIFT TO US

AGNES CHAMPAGNE

TEACH Services, Inc.
P U B L I S H I N G
www.TEACHServices.com • (800) 367-1844

Copyright© 2023 Agnes Champagne
Copyright© 2023 TEACH Services, Inc.
ISBN-13: 978-1-4796-1551-3 (Paperback)
ISBN-13: 978-1-4796-1552-0 (ePub)
Library of Congress Control Number: 2023908404

All scripture quotations, unless otherwise indicated, are taken from the Holy Bible, King James Version (Public Domain).

TEACH Services, Inc.
P U B L I S H I N G
www.TEACHServices.com • (800) 367-1844

TABLE OF CONTENTS

CHAPTER ONE

As I tell my story, I will begin with what I can remember as a child, as I grew up, and what the Lord has done and is doing in my life. I always feared the Lord as I grew up, but I did not know why. Growing up, my parents always taught us to take care of ourselves; I did not realize someone out there could help me and love me. I always felt I was missing something in my life. I knew it was the love of God after I started reading the Bible. I ran across a verse that says Jesus is coming again to get his people. A verse in Deuteronomy says: "Thou shalt fear the Lord thy God; him shalt thou serve, and to Him shalt thou cleave, and swear by his name" (Deut. 10:20, KJV). A verse in Luke states: "And he said to them all, If any man will come after me, let him deny himself, and take up his cross daily, and follow me" (Luke 9:23, KJV). When your fate brings you to the Lord, he will be there for you. Another verse in Philippians tells us: "I can do all things through Christ which strengtheneth me" (Phil. 4:13, KJV). A verse in Jeremiah says, "They are turned back to the iniquities of their forefathers, which refused to hear my words…" (Jer. 11:10, KJV).

As I studied the Word of God, I knew my commitment should be serving the Lord. I believe God has a plan for his people. By serving God, the Holy Spirit will lead you to the truth. I am from a family of ten children. My mother lost a set of twins, a boy, and a girl. After they were born, when I first saw them, I had names picked out for them. Unfortunately, the doctors could not respond fast enough, and my parents lost them after a few hours. My parents had a large family of eleven children. I was the third to be born in the family. Their oldest son decided he did not want to work on the farm, so he decided to join CCC Camp. It was not easy to make a living back then. We were very, very poor, and we had to work hard to make a living. My parents had no education and spoke only French. We farmed for a living until my teenage years. My mother's dad always lived with us because he lost his wife when my mother was born. When my mother asked to get married, he asked my dad if he could live with them.

He always lived with us, and was a good grandpa to us. As a child, my siblings and I did not have many toys; instead, we had to reuse old toys. I remember when my father would dig a well to get water, and he would make us clay dolls. For the boys, he would make balls. He would garden and help my mother with the youngest children. We had fun picking up the eggs together, and we would race to see which one picked up the most. At age twelve and thirteen, I remember Dad taking me to the fields to teach me how to hoe cotton, corn, and sugarcane. He trained us to pick cotton at a very young age. The younger ones would get on the other side of the rows so we could watch and teach them how to pick cotton. When the sugarcanes were ready to be cut, I would go with my dad to cut the canes, lay them in rows, and stack them, ready to load in the wagon. Then, I would have to go to the wagon to catch a bundle of the canes, and when the wagon was full, he would take it to the refinery. We only possessed two cows; I remember we did not always have milk. We did not have doughnuts and milk for breakfast; we had a good old cornbread and syrup, hot biscuits with jam, and homemade butter, sometimes with a glass of water. Occasionally, we were allowed a treat.

My grandpa would get free commodities. He would get whole wheat flour, sugar, grits, corn meal, and powdered milk. Mother would add those to the kitchen. One thing that helped us was my mother's canning in jars. She would put away the extra food we could not eat, and we would have it with soups from the garden in the winter months. She made delicious old French soup recipes. When she had enough flour, we would have hot biscuits, and we never complained because we were eating delicious food. My older sister did not work in the field much. Instead, she helped her mother in the kitchen. I was assigned to the garden while my father worked in the cotton field. My older sister and I would pick cotton. The younger ones would bring lemonade and water to drink while they worked in the field. I learned how to cook from my mother. I also learned how to sew by observing my mother. The neighbors would bring her old catalogs; she would let us pick out which dress we wanted her to make. She would use newspapers from the neighbors to cut a pattern to make clothing.

Going back to school days, we were a couple of miles from neighbors with children that spoke English.

Speaking with those children helped us learn a little English before we attended school. I was a shy little girl. When I started school, the town girls had many friends, but I had only a couple. I remember one little girl who kept talking to me, and one day, she said my mother and father adopted me, but over time, she became my friend. She would bring candy and cookies to school and share them with me. After a while, she said it was my turn to bring candy, but I knew I did not have any money. I remembered my mother put a bill in the chest of drawers, so I looked for it, and it was still there. I took the bill in the morning, stopped at the store and told the owner I wanted two candy bars. I gave him the bill, and he asked where I got it. I told him I got it from my house and found it in the chest of drawers. He responded by handing me the candy bars and my change. He then told me to make sure I gave it back to my parents. He knew my dad would not buy candies for us often. My mom would always hand-make our sweet treats. When I returned home, my dad already knew about the missing bill because he went to the store for something he needed the same day, so when I returned from school, dad asked me for the change. I gave it to him. My mother heard the discussion; she entered the room in tears. I'd never seen my mother cry before. I remember she asked my dad how much I spent at the store. He told her it was not enough to hurt their financial situation. She asked if they had enough money left to buy flour, to which he responded, "yes." I thought I was going to get disciplined, but I did not. I never saw my dad spank any of us. He would take his razor leather strap out, and that was it. However, he admonished me for what seemed like hours. I remember him saying: "We always taught our children never to take anything that did not belong to you, even from the house, without asking. I was ashamed of my actions; I kept apologizing to my mother. I knew it was likely we would not have enough flour for cakes. When we had enough flour, she would make us cookies or cakes. Another treat she would make was bread pudding with leftover bread, and when she did not have enough bread, she would use carrots or white squash; it was just as good as a regular cake. I kept asking my mom if there was enough money to buy flour. That experience hurt me, and I learned my lesson. As I grew older, I realized we had good parents. They feared God and taught us how to fear God as well. They say always do what is right, and you will stay out of trouble.

CHAPTER TWO

My parents taught us to share and help others. In my early days, my parents never learned about God; they just went to church when they could. I can remember my brother and sister walking a mile and a half to go to the Catholic Church. I always felt like I never got anything out of church because the priest would speak Latin, and I could not understand anything he said. I asked my mother why they spoke Latin because I did not understand. Education was not much fun for me. I was slow when it came to learning English. By the time I got to the fifth grade, it was easier for me. I attended school regularly until seventh grade, but in the eighth grade, my dad desperately needed help, and it was a hit and miss that year. I decided to drop out and work to help out. Most of us were already grown, so we needed more food and clothing. At the age of fourteen, I got a job as a babysitter. My uncle's friends knew a couple that needed help with their children on weekends. I decided to go because they knew I could do the job. My uncle told them I would be a good babysitter.

They would pick me up on Friday evening and bring me back on Sunday evening. I would babysit a three-year-old and a one-year-old. I would play with them, feed them, and change the youngest's old diaper, and

I would often get up at night if the baby cried. They gave me three dollars for the job. The money I got was helpful because it allowed me to help my dad. After all, he was still farming. Back in those days, the boys would make fun of the girls because we wore homemade cloth and torn socks. When I told my mother, she said they didn't know they shouldn't make fun of others because they have no respect. She told me not to give them attention, and they would stop. She said she would not be surprised if they do not get away with that at home. She said, "I hope you won't ever do that. That is why we teach you all to do what is right, and you will stay out of trouble."

One day, the home economics teacher said she could teach us how to darn our socks. She instructed us to take a hard ball and run the sock through it, and then she would demonstrate the process. I learned to darn socks so we would not have to wear torn socks anymore. As you can see, there was always someone to help us. My older sister quit school in the ninth grade. Our first job was in a restaurant. We knew the parents of a couple who owned a restaurant. My sister and I went to work there, and our job was in the kitchen to chop onion, celery, bell pepper, and other vegetables for the cooks. The second year, they offered to allow us to work in the kitchen, and when we were ready to open up, they allowed us to wait on tables. They told us it would give us a chance to make more money. However, we enjoyed working in the kitchen there; their parents worked in the kitchen, too. We called our boss "mom mom" because she was like a grandma to us. By the time my sister and I had saved two hundred dollars each, we agreed to share it with dad.

One day, we went into town and saw a house for sale. We called the number on the sign and asked how much the owner wanted for it. They told us it was forty-eight thousand dollars. The man said it needed repairs and he was too old to do it himself. We knew it was big enough for our family. At the time, there were seven children, and my grandpa and my dad's brother moved in with us. He was previously living with my grandpa, but he passed away. We explained the house to my dad to see if he wanted to look at it. When he saw it, he said he thought it would work for us; however, we had a lot of work to do. Dad told us we needed a down payment. We later called the man and asked how much money we would need down, and he asked us how much we already had. We told him four hundred dollars. He said it was enough, and he could finance it for my family.

There was a canning factory not far from the house. My siblings and I told dad he could stop farming and see if the canning factory would hire him. They desperately needed workers, so they hired him. My uncle also decided he wanted a job, and they hired him. The following week my sister-in-law went for an interview; she received the job not long after. The manager asked my dad if he knew anyone who needed a job. My dad told him he had another young daughter. They told him to bring me in, and I got the job. We were all trained for the job, and all along, my dad knew I could do it.

CHAPTER THREE

When I was old enough, I went to work at the dime store. I worked there until it burned down. After it burned down, another dime store offered all of us jobs. I went to work there, and after one year, they called me into the office and offered me an office job. I asked the man what the job would entail; he told me I would check freight when it arrived, count the money out of the money bags, count the change, and get it wrapped up. I told the man I would give it a shot. He was confident that I could do the job. I did not know the other girls did not like that idea very much because they had graduated, and they knew I had not. It felt good to have my own money, but I was more worried about doing quality work. I worked in the office for about two years. The store had a little breakfast bar; I would always go to work early and would sometimes sit at the bar and have toast. There was a lady that would come in every day for coffee. We would always chat until it was time for me to go to the office. I learned she owned a dress shop not far from the dime store.

One day she said, "Would you like to come to work for me? I'm by myself, and I need help. I have a good business." I told her I was not certain I could sell clothes. She told me I had a nice personality and was

capable of the position. She informed me that she would train me, so I told her I would think about it, and the following day, I took her up on her offer. She said when the business increases I would be able to train the new girl. The woman had a nice expensive clothing shop. She would help me get my clothes at wholesale prices, so I could wear the clothes we sold. I enjoyed my work there very much. The woman treated me like a daughter that she never had. At nineteen, I did not go out much and did not have a boyfriend. Mom and dad had friends that had only one boy my age; my parents and his parents had been friends for a long time. Those friends had other relatives, and between all of us, we would get together and play ball. The couple with one boy decided to move to New Orleans. They went to work for a shipyard company, so mom and dad lost contact with them. There were not many people with phones or nice cars. The son had joined the service at a young age. One day, my dad informed us they moved back. I immediately told him that I wanted to visit. He let me go with him and let me drive. I had just received my license, so I agreed. We had a pleasant visit. When the son returned from work, we looked at each other; he said, "I can't believe what I am seeing. It's good to see you."

He asked me to go to the living room. He showed me where he had been, and we caught up with each other. He later asked my dad if he could bring me home that night. Three weeks passed before I heard from him again. One day after work, he came by. He said he would visit every evening he could. It took him one month before he asked me out to supper one night. We dated for eight months before we got engaged. Four months later, we married. My husband and I had a wonderful life; we raised three children, two boys, and one girl. We were married for fifty-nine and a half years before I lost him. We had our trials as well. My husband knew how to work hard, and so did I. He worked for an insurance company for a couple of years. He did extremely well, but they kept taking policies. One day, he told me the company was growing but wanted to make more money.

My husband told me he was looking for something he could call his own business. One day, he was reading the newspaper and saw a listing for a semi-professional business for a husband and wife team. He called the number, and it was to fit hearing aids. Even though he knew nothing about it, he promised to train us. We took the offer and stayed in business for thirty-three and a half years. The first few years in business were hard. I later decided to go to beauty school. The old house we had bought was big enough to have both businesses at home. The arrangement worked well, and I was able to take care of both businesses. I did hair for thirty years. Somehow, the Lord was working things out for us. We never got rich but always made enough to pay and clear all our bills. We did not owe anything. We never bought what we could not afford; things have changed today. You cannot say it is the good old days anymore. We did not know much about God; we just feared and wanted to do things right.

One Sunday, as I was doing my chores in the house, I was listening to the television, and I heard a man talk about the Sabbath. He discussed keeping it because it was one of the commandments; it is Holy. He said there is nothing holy about Sunday. It is the first day of the week. Saturday is the seventh day. It is also the day God says He rested on, and sanctified it; therefore, it is holy. When my husband came in from the yard, we discussed it. He said the man was right. We found it interesting and wanted to know more about it. At that time, we were not attending Church. We had stopped going to the Catholic Church because they had things going on that were against our beliefs. We did not think it was right, so we turned to the Bible.

Our Bible sat on the shelf for a long time, collecting dust. We started studying the commandments; it told us to remember to keep the Sabbath day Holy and to remember a very impartment word in The Bible. He did not want us to forget. He used the word 'remember' at the last supper as well. He said to do this in remembrance of him. He did not want them to forget either. The next step was to close our business on Sabbath day, and then we started looking for a church that keeps the Sabbath. We found one listed in the phone book, so we decided to take a ride. When we arrived, we saw they were building it. My husband talked to a couple of men; they said we could talk to the pastor. He was working on the Church too. He said it would most likely be open in a month. We waited a month and a half before we went to Church.

CHAPTER FOUR

We attended the service and were very impressed. We noticed the Church was teaching the truth. We studied The Bible with them. We were blessed, and things began to happen in our lives like never before. I began to notice the Lord was working in our lives. My husband would stay in the office until ten in the morning and make house calls. When the clients did not show up, he ran a test in their homes. One night, he was late coming home. I had gone to bed and put the pillows behind my back as I read, waiting for him to return. The phone rang, and he knew he was late, but assured me he was okay. He told me he hit a horse in the road, busted the windshield, and would have to drive slow. In the meantime, I read all of Luke and Matthew.

I began to relax, so I decided to lay down and get some rest while waiting on my husband. I could not go to sleep because I was restless. I started talking to the Lord. I often went to the bathroom and looked at the clock. It was just after midnight. I jumped in bed and kept repeating the time, then stopped for a second and started again louder this time. I asked the Lord what was happening as Revelation made a loud noise in my mind. I asked the Lord if he wanted me to find Rev. 12:12.

I opened my Bible and read. "Therefore rejoice, ye heavens, and ye that dwell in them. Woe to the inhabiters of the earth and of the sea! For the devil is come down unto you, having great wrath, because he knoweth that he hath but a short time" (Rev. 12:12, KJV). I reread it and could not believe what I was reading. I asked if He was trying to tell me the devil was out to get me. Since we studied before, we knew what the devil was trying to do to God's people. Look what he did to Eve. When I felt things were off, I called on God, and the devil was unsuccessful. I have been so thankful to God for allowing me to understand how the devil works.

That was my first encounter with the Lord. I did not know He would give me more parables from The Bible. The experience brought us closer to the Lord, and we decided to live a Bible Christian life. A few months later, he gave me a verse from Psalms. I set my clock for five. When I looked at the clock, it was forty-seven minutes after four. I stayed in bed until the clock rang. In the meantime, all I could see in my mind was forty-four and seven. Reflecting on the first experience, I picked up my Bible and asked God where I could find 44:7. He responded by telling me to open my Bible. After He repeated it, I opened my Bible and searched for Psalms. I turned the pages until I found the verse God directed me to. "But thou hast saved us from our enemies, and hast put them to shame that hated us" (Ps. 44:7, KJV).

God is full of surprises. He gives His people what they need. My prayers would always include the bad people and the good. We have so much to be thankful for. I realized that there was only one out there that could do it for me. He is a living God, and He loves all people, but he hates sin. No one else can take his place. He knows each of us, and He can work miracles for his people. We were so thankful that he was guiding us in the right direction. I would set my clock half an hour earlier every day to read my Bible and talk to the Lord. It was worth it because He kept blessing us. We can go to him and tell him our needs because we need His help. Once you confess your sins, The Bible says your sins are forgiven but to sin no more. When He starts blessing you, tell someone.

We can never say there is no hope. He can provide a way out. It is the sacrifice He made for us. All we need is faith. He has a plan for each one of us. His word will be preached, and everyone will hear the truth before He comes back, but they will have to choose whose side they will be on. There will only be two sides, the righteous and the unrighteous. A few verses that come to my mind come from Isaiah and Proverbs. "Seek ye the Lord while he may be found, call ye upon him while he is near ..." (Isa. 55:6, KJV). "He that turneth away his ear from hearing the law, even his prayer shall be abomination" (Prov. 28:9, KJV). Verse thirteen says, "He that covereth his sins shall not prosper: but whoso confesseth and forsaketh them shall have mercy" (Prov. 28:13, KJV). "But he turned, and said unto Peter, Get thee behind me, Satan ..." (Matt. 16:23, KJV). Mark 8:35–38 discusses what purpose a man if he shall gain the whole world and lose his soul; "Whosoever therefore shall be ashamed of me and of my words in this adulterous and sinful generation; of him all shall the Son of man be ashamed, when he cometh in the glory of his Father with the holy angels" (Mark 8:38, KJV).

Everyone is a child of God; He created us. He needs all the respect we can give Him, and He loves us all, but He has conditions. God gave us free will; we can choose whom we will serve, but He is the only one who can cleanse us from our sins; God can give us hope when there is no hope; peace when there is no peace, knowledge, and wisdom. If we do not serve him, then we will find ourselves in this world without peace. Our pleasure could become our God. The only prayer He gave us in The Bible is The Lord's Prayer. We should meditate on it more often. Our lives today have been completely turned around.

> **"**
> God gave us free will; we can choose whom we will serve, but He is the only one who can cleanse us from our sins; God can give us hope when there is no hope; peace when there is no peace, knowledge, and wisdom.
> **"**

The Bible says we are in a time of trouble. We should be ready now so we can get the faith we need to go through the trouble times that will soon come upon us. Anyone can find the time to talk and pray to God if they choose. It is also very important to keep all of His Commandments. The fourth commandment says to remember and not forget. Most people keep Sunday, but no one can change His word or add anything to it because His name is taken out of the book of life. We cannot add or take away what we do not want; there is nothing with the word of God that does not make sense.

It is perfect, and it details important events and what we will see happen before Jesus comes to get His people. You can also find out which day changed in the book. "He that is unjust, let him be unjust still: and he which is filthy, let him be filthy still: and he that is righteous, let him be righteous still: and he that is holy, let him be holy still" (Rev. 22:11, KJV). "And, behold, I come quickly; and my reward is with me, to give every man according as his work shall be" (Rev. 22:12, KJV). He loves us so much that He left instructions for us to follow. What we give up for his sake, we will never lose. When we find the Lord, we can climb one step at a time, but if we do not seek him, we go down one step at a time.

Many verses in The Bible that say if we love Him, keep his commandments. Our bodies are not our own; we are the temple of the Holy Spirit. Our parents could not teach us the word of God because no one was teaching them the word of God. Everyone was told to keep the Sunday. Some never learned about God; they believed The Bible was not a book to be read. I remember a few times we would walk to our neighbor, and she had a French Bible she would read to us. We always enjoyed that, but I am thankful that our parents kept us on the right track with what they knew was right and wrong.

CHAPTER FIVE

Things have changed from my time to now. Is it for the best? People are busy with phones and computers. Almost every two-year-old has a phone or laptop. There is not much family life anymore; both parents have to work. I do not see that it works out because families often spend more money than they make. Debts have skyrocketed. About fifty years ago, there was family life. I do not see much of that today. Spending more time with my Bible, I can see that God is giving me more light, and my faith has increased. God said, "Blessed are the eyes which see the things that ye see …" (Luke 10:23, KJV). There are many things people desire but are not willing to hear His words. We must learn to put the old self away and walk in the light He gives us. Like a song says, "I want to be part of the family of God." Some like to watch dirty movies or scary movies, sit and eat unhealthy food, or have fun with a laptop. They go where they have lots of excitement. I am not trying to insult anyone; I did some of that until the Lord gave me light. I soon realized that giving it up was a blessing.

My hobbies are cooking, sewing, and most of all, painting. I did China painting for many years, now as I'm painting in oil, a verse came to my mind in Mark.

"Whoever will come after Me, let him deny himself, and take up his cross, and follow me" (Mark 8:34, KJV). God is waiting to give us all the blessings we need; all we have to do is go to Him. He tells us to ask, and we shall receive, and to knock, and the door will open. We need all the blessings we can get because the world is a place of confusion. Some people cannot seem to get it straight. There is no confusion around serving God. You can bank on his word. Some people forget God created Adam and Eve and told them to have offspring. God says killing an unborn baby is wrong. He tells us to never kill. Going back to the fourth Commandment it has his seal, name, and title. He is our creator, and Satan is a liar. He is working very hard today to keep the truth from the light. I am taking a stand for God with the light he has given me. "For by grace are ye saved through faith; and that not of yourselves: it is the gift of God" (Eph. 2:8, KJV). "Whosoever committeth sin transgresseth also the law: for sin is the transgression of the law" (1 John 3:4, KJV).

In Exodus, it says, "Thou shall have no other gods before me." (Exod. 20:3, KJV). If we love God, we will put no other gods before him. We will all get trials, but we must hang on, go to God and put things in His hands. He will give us victory. Our earth is decaying, and we have a sin problem. The devil is hard at work, especially with our children. We must remember God wrote the Ten Commandments on stone. The first four describe duty to God, and the last six are duty to his fellow man. Today, you can see what Satan is doing to marriage, as he is trying to destroy the Sabbath. I like what it says in Matthew, "Go ye therefore, and teach all nations … Teaching them to observe all things whatsoever I have commanded you: and, lo, I am with you always, even unto the end of the world" (Matt. 28:19–20, KJV). Revelation 18 says, "Come out of her, my people, that ye be not partakers of her sins, and that ye receive not of her plagues" (Rev. 18:4, KJV). In Isaiah, He says, "I am the Lord thy God, the Holy One" (Isa. 43:3, KJV).

Remember, I am not writing my story to insult anyone. I hope it will help others see God's love. We will need God's love and more faith moving forward. We want to enjoy Heaven and what He has in store for us. Like the song says, "What a day that will be. There will never be sin, sickness, no more killing or wars, and no more rich or poor." Satan keeps trying to discourage me, but God keeps giving me more light. He gave me a verse in Jeremiah, "Call unto me, and I will answer thee, and show thee great and mighty things, which thou knowest not" (Jer. 33:3, KJV). This is the kind of God we serve; He is faithful and should be first. Another verse in Psalms says, "Thou lovest righteousness and hatest wickedness; therefore God, Thy God, hath anointed Thee with the oil of gladness …" (Ps. 45:7, KJV). I keep praying for all the unrighteous people out there. If they would stop and call on God, they could have a change of heart and would experience the love He has for them. He wants to save as many as He can. Our sin keeps us weak, and we need Him to cleanse us. He tells us to come to him as we are.

A few months later, He blessed me with another verse in Psalm, "The angel of the Lord encampeth round about them that fear him, and delivereth them" (Ps. 34:7, KJV). When I feared God, I did not know Him, and now I fear God *because* I know him. I know what He expects of me. He is giving me light, and He says to share it. God is our refuge and strength; He can give us the strength we need. Another parable he gave me is in Psalm 55, "Fearfulness and trembling are come upon me, and horror hath overwhelmed me" (Ps. 55:5, KJV). Satan loves to keep us on his side. I was in the doctor's hands, and they could not solve my problem. Sure, it brought me down, but I did not stay there. I called on God, the living God who could hear me. The next day, I felt better and knew God would take care of things. Two days later, I went to my heart doctor. He said he thought I needed a pacemaker. The following week, I went to a doctor for the procedure. I had surgery, and all went well—I recovered quickly. Two months later, I had a red spot where the pacemaker was placed. I called the doctor and made an appointment. I went in, he looked at it, and he said it was infected. He administered antibiotics and said I would have to come back if it did not clear up, because then it would have to be removed. I went home and started talking to the Lord. I told Him all went well, and it healed fine. I put things in His hands. The next day, He gave me another parable in Psalms. "For he hath delivered me out of all trouble: and mine eye hath seen his desire upon mine enemies" (Ps. 54:7, KJV). God always sends us what we need. My experiences have increased my faith so much that it's hard to describe the feeling. I wish whoever reads my story can experience the feeling that you can never go wrong by serving God. I will always call upon God, and the Lord shall save me. What an awesome God we serve! An experience like that is the most precious gift you can have. He will never leave or forsake us. In Isaiah, it says, "Surely he hath borne our griefs, and carried our sorrows: yet we did esteem him stricken, smitten of God, and afflicted" (Isa. 53:4, KJV).

CHAPTER SIX

In 2 Chronicles, it says, "If my people, which are called by my name, shall humble themselves, and pray, and seek my face, and turn from their wicked ways; then will I hear from heaven, and will forgive their sin, and will heal their land" (2 Chron. 7:14, KJV). I remember reading, "The Lord is my helper, and I will not fear what man shall do unto me" (Heb. 13:6, KJV). "He sent his word, and healed them, and delivered them from their destructions" (Ps. 107:20, KJV). Most of these verses come from Psalm. I have read it so many times; God knows I like it. I can claim all his promises, and I understand it better. I never get tired of reading it. Of course, I have read all the others many times. When I first found the Lord, I would write Him letters. I had found out how to talk to Him to express my feelings.

I have included a portion of the letter. With God's grace, we can overcome. We have hope, and we have assurance. All we have to do is give him our hearts so he can cleanse us. I feel so hurt when I talk to people about God, and they do not show interest. Sometimes, they will cut you short and start talking about something else. God will not do that; my letter to the Lord. It all started four and a half years ago. Remember that night coming back from the restaurant we both went to You in prayer? We went up the steps and did not know how to come down. We were hurting bad. The hurt was coming from people we loved. We wore a smile, but we were crying from our hearts, and it hurts. We felt strange and did not have much feeling for anything. While finding ourselves going to You, we realized that You had been hurt many times too. When the doors opened for us that day, we felt like our lives were starting over, and they were. We were like born-again Christians.

The doors opened that year, and we sough God for the truth. We talked about God; we knew that was the only direction to go. In the second year, we picked up our faith and learned more about God. We were still hurting, but we knew we could not turn back. We kept on looking. We attended many churches. In the third year, we received more light, still seeking, and many questions. We still received more light, and one day our Pastor came to our rescue with Bible lessons. By the fourth year, we were witnessing to others and marching on. Looking up to You, going to You in pain, and giving You our hearts to be healed. You gave us patience; You healed us, and something began to happen. Something was taking place in our lives. We were transformed into new people. We did not have time for hurt, self-pity, or blaming each other for what went wrong. We found ourselves praying for one another and praying for those who had hurt us. We were involved with You. We are forgiving others and have stopped judging, and you are healing us. Now, it does not hurt as much.

We put matters in your hands and understood. We are not all bad, but as Psalm puts it, we are rotten to the core. We were sick people, each in our separate way. We are getting well but not cured. We are still taking treatment, but we learned if we could not pray for those who hurt us, we need to pray for ourselves because, as Matthew puts it, "And forgive us our debts, as we forgive us our debtors" (Matt. 6:12, KJV). We are getting closer and closer to You by the day. We are allowing more time for You; we are allowing You to accomplish Your work in us. We know now that if things do not go right, it is not Your fault. We know we should go back and see where we went wrong. The more time we spend with You, the easier it is for us to see our faults. We have the patience to solve our problems. You see, as we are growing in faith, our hurt is going away. It does not hurt as much as four and a half years ago. We are so lucky to have found you together. The way I feel this evening, I could talk and write to You forever. We are lucky to have found a Father, a friend, and a God all in one.

By the hand, it is left up to us to go to Him. We have free will. I am so glad to look forward to my new home like the song says, "This world is not my home. Our world today is falling apart. Soon, He will come to take us home." In the 60s, we were involved in a bad accident. Five young boys drove around a curve after they had been drinking and hit us head-on. They took us to the hospital to check us out and discharged us when they felt we could go home. My husband was not hurt; however, two days later, I went into a coma. They brought me back to the hospital, and I would just scream. They took x-rays and did not see anything. I stayed in a coma for seven days. When I woke up, they ran into my room. They asked where I was hurting, and I told them in my neck. The x-rays showed a crushed neck bone in my upper back. I can thank God that my recovery went well.

I had many close calls in my life. When I look at it, I call it a miracle. God always saw me through. Another miracle happened when I attended a fifteen-day program at the Wild Wood Center. While there, they noticed I was having heart problems, so they made an appointment for me at a heart hospital. They checked me out and said I had a blockage in my heart. I came back home and called friends in Florida. He was doing pastoral work there at the hospital. We told them what they found, and he said I needed to take a plane and come here to see a doctor; he had just had a bypass. The next day we get on a plane, and he picked us up at the airport. He made me an appointment with his doctor the next day. We had a pleasant visit and prayed a lot, and I went to bed at eleven. The men stayed and chatted. I could not sleep as usual because I was talking to the Lord. Immediately, I saw an arrow and felt it go from left to right through my heart. I was stung. I felt like a good feeling came upon me. I got up at four in the morning; my appointment was at five. Our friends, Pastor Erny Roy and his wife, Mary, lived on the hospital grounds; we did not have far to go. They ran the test, and it showed no blockage. I told the doctor what happened, and I felt the Lord had taken care of it.

He says, "according to your records, someone took care of it for you." I had many close calls. Praise God! He always took care of me, and He continues to do so. After thirty-three and a half years of hard work, we retired. We were only in our early fifties. We figured if

we could sell the house and office, it would be enough for us to retire. We both worked hard, long hours all our lives, so we thought it was time to slow down. We made our decisions and put the house for sale. We sold it ourselves. We knew a couple, and my husband talked to him and his wife. They came to see the house and immediately fell in love with it. My husband said he could train them. He said, "Well, that might work out because I was ready to give this job up." In the meantime, we were looking for something to get for retirement. My brother lived in Alabama, so he called to tell us they had a house and forty acres for auction the following week.

We did not know if we wanted that much land, but it was worth looking at. We arranged to visit and made our bid.

We were able to have two big gardens; we did not get any animals. We made all we could use and shared what we could not eat. We enjoyed that for twelve years until my husband's mother fell ill. Being the only child, we decided to come back home, which was to Louisiana. When we were ready to sell our home in Alabama, we gave it to three different real estate companies, and they never could sell it. We told them it was enough, and we would try and sell it ourselves. We ran an ad, and luckily, many calls came in. We made three appointments for the following Sunday so they could come to see it. When the first couple came, they liked it very much. They left and said they would check back. Before they left, the second couple came, but they did not think they could afford it but considered it since they could sell some of their property. When they left, the third couple came and liked it very much. At the same time, the first couple asked us to hold the property for them. We could not believe what was going on. The husband looked at me and said, "isn't the Lord good?" He says the real estate company had it for six months and did not do anything with it. I am telling you all this because this is how God works with his people. He will not let you down if you serve him. I have many more stories to talk about how God worked in our life when we put him first. I am sure many of you who will read my book will sound familiar to you because you have had the same experience. God is so good, so we need to tell others.

CHAPTER SEVEN

Going back to selling our house and the business, we had three small houses for rent. We were on one corner of the block and the three little houses on the other corner. When our bid went through, we asked if we could first give him enough money to tie the deal down, and he agreed. We told him we had three houses we could sell and would take care of the sale. He agreed to that, too. One got sold, so we went to give him the money. We told him as soon as the other one sells, then we will be back. We sold the third one and had enough to pay him out. We went to the lawyer to close the deal. He heard the story and said, "You did that with just a handshake?" He could not believe it. We knew the seller was being honest, and I guess he knew we were honest.

Once more, Satan was trying to pull me down. I sat in my chair talking to the Lord. One morning, I looked at the clock; the time was eleven minutes after eleven. I thought to myself, *It will soon be time for lunch*. After a few minutes, I kept seeing eleven eleven. I repeated it, and again, I could see it so clear. It occurred six or seven years after He had given me another verse. It had been a long time. I said, "Lord, You are bringing me back to the Bible, and You know I have been reading more." I asked

Him about the numbers, and He said to open the Bible. I retrieved my Bible and opened it up, and I lowered my chair to get in a better position. Immediately, I felt such a heavy cloud come over me. It was dark, and by the time it got to my toes, it was white. It started in my head. Then, a warm feeling came from my head to my toes. Then, I felt so full of the Holy Spirit; it was a feeling that I cannot explain. I started crying. I felt so good. I just stayed there for a while. I called my friend and told her about the experience. Going back to my Bible, I opened it but did not look at it. It was right at the beginning of Psalms. I looked at it, but there was no verse eleven. I looked at two, and it had an eleventh verse in it.

Before I went further, I needed to talk with the Holy Spirit.

Every time I would pray for someone, I would call on the Holy Spirit. You see, the Holy Spirit is real. The Holy Spirit took the place of Jesus when He left to go to His father. The Holy Spirit was left to comfort us; we can go to it for everything else. God did not leave us without help. God, the Father, and the Holy Spirit work together. We have not been abandoned. Praise his name, and God will give us so many surprises. I received my answer. Going back to my Bible, I opened it to Psalm. "Serve the Lord with fear, and rejoice with trembling" (Ps. 2:11, KJV). When I reread, I still saw it clearly. I said, "Lord, do You want me to read more?" A thought came to my mind, so I read again. I continued to read more of Psalm. "But let all those that put their trust in thee rejoice: let them ever shout for joy, because thou defendest them: let them also that love thy name be joyful in thee" (Ps. 5:11, KJV).

We have to be ready for Christ to return. We should stay prepared because we do not know the hour or the day. Moving to Psalm 7, "God judges the righteous, and God is angry with the wicked everyday" (Ps. 7:11, KJV). We should trust God to help us through our trials, and if we truly follow Him, the reward is great, and He will deliver us from evil. "Sing praises to the Lord, which dwelleth in Zion: declare among the people his doings (Ps. 9:11, KJV). God deserves our Praise; He wants me to tell my story. Every time I start reading, I read something that leads me to tell my story. Psalm 10 says, "He hath said in his heart, God hath forgotten: he hideth his face; he will never see it. We cannot depend on ourselves; we have to depend on God. When God is present, there is no room for pride. Psalm 17 says, "They have now compassed us in our steps: they have set their eyes bowing down to earth" (Ps. 17:11, KJV). We can surround ourselves with others and boast with pride and lose God. The devil is fast in leading us in that direction. The Lord knew what He could help me with.

I kept asking him, and He gave me the answer. When that cloud came over me as I kept repeating eleven eleven, I know he wanted me to read and talk about it. I would be a witness for Him. This was not the first time He gave me parables in the Bible; the others I have learned. However, when I read it, some of them I can read without looking at them. I have read them so many times. I included a little explanation with each parable as the Lord was guiding me. I can pray and hope it will help someone else like it has helped me. As our time gets shorter on earth, He will reveal much more to His people. No one will be left out without hearing his word. We have experienced a big challenge in the last two years, and it is just the beginning of the time of trouble the Lord talks about in the Bible. It is in Daniel, Mark, Luke, Matthew, Revelation, and many others.

He made darkness his secret place; His pavilion round about him were dark waters and thick clouds of the skies" (Ps. 18:11, KJV). God gives protection to us; like the mother chicken protects her chicks. We can bank on that. When He sees we are in trouble, He will provide. "Moreover by them is thy servant warned: and in keeping of them there is great reward"

(Ps. 19:11, KJV). God's laws protect us from danger. The Commandments help to make us wise so we can enjoy life. "For they intended evil against thee: they imagined a mischievous device, which they are not able to perform" (Ps. 21:11, KJV). We should respect God's love because He knew us before birth. What more can we ask for? "Be not far from me; for trouble is near; for there is none to help" (Ps. 22:11, KJV). There is only God; He can help us in trouble. That's why we need to stay close to him. "For thy name's sake, O Lord, pardon my iniquity; for it is great" (Ps. 25:11, KJV). God is eternal, Holy, and above all else. He wants to guide us so we can make it to Heaven—our forever home.

"But as for me, I will walk in mine integrity: redeem me, and be merciful unto me" (Ps. 26:11, KJV). As sinful people, we should walk in the light He can give us. "Teach me thy way, O Lord, and lead me in a plain path, because of mine enemies" (Ps. 27:11, KJV). We are children of God; He can lead and guide us to the right path. He can keep our enemies away as well. "The Lord will give strength unto his people; the Lord will bless his people with peace" (Ps. 29:11, KJV). God has the power to raise the dead. He raised Christ. When we are weak, remember He can pick us up. "Thou has turned for me my mourning into dancing: thou hast put off my sackcloth, and girded me with gladness" (Ps. 30:11, KJV). Praise God for His mercy.

Serving God does not make us sad. He can deliver us from our sadness. "I was a reproach among all mine enemies, but especially among my neighbors, and a fear to mine acquaintance: they that did see me without fled from me" (Ps. 31:11, KJV). Sometimes, we feel like someone hates us. Remember, if they hate you, they are hopeless. We can take courage because God is watching out for us. "Be glad in the Lord, and rejoice, ye righteous: and shout for joy, all ye that are upright in heart" (Ps. 32:11, KJV). God longs to guide us so we can work for Him. He knows what is best for our lives. That tells us how much love he has for us. Another verse in Psalm says, "The counsel of the Lord standeth forever, the thoughts of his heart to all generations" (Ps. 33:11, KJV). God's plans do not change. His promises come to us from him, so we should let God do the work in us. That would make Him very happy. "Come, ye children, hearken unto me: I will teach you the fear of the Lord" (Ps. 34:11, KJV). Like The Bible says, fear God, and keep His commandments. If we fear God, then we will turn away from sin, and we will do something good instead, and we will obey Him.

CHAPTER EIGHT

"False witnesses did rise up; they laid to my charge things that I knew not" (Ps. 35:11, KJV). Our trials will come, but we have to stand for the Lord. God's command is for our good. God will rescue us with open arms. "Let not the foot of pride come against me, and let not the hand of the wicked remove me" (Ps. 36:11, KJV). God's holiness stretches out of His hand to keep us from falling. He spoke of himself as living water and eternal life. I want to drink that water, don't you? "But the meek shall inherit the earth; and shall delight themselves in the abundance of peace" (Ps. 37:11, KJV). Faith gives us hope, and hope can deliver us. He has a reward for people; you never look back when you serve him. "My lovers and my friends stand aloof from my sore; and my kinsmen stand afar off" (Ps. 38:11, KJV). God hears the desires of our hearts. He wants us to hear His message so he can prepare us for the Heavenly Kingdom. "When thou with rebukes dost correct man for iniquity, thou makest his beauty to consume away like a moth: surely every man is vanity. Selah" (Ps. 39:11, KJV).

We have to ask God to hear our prayers and be careful in which direction we are heading in. "Withhold not thou thy tender mercies from me, O Lord: let thy lovingkindness and thy truth continually preserve me" (Ps. 40:11, KJV). When God blesses us, we should share with others what He has done for us. We should not be ashamed to tell what He has done for us. "By this I know that thou favourest me, because mine enemy doth not triumph over me" (Ps. 41:11, KJV). Praise God for His goodness. He takes care of his people. "Why are thou cast down, O my soul? and why art thou disquieted within me? Hope thou in God: for I shall yet praise him, who is the health of my countenance, and my God" (Ps. 42:11, KJV). We should keep our minds focused on God. Meditate on his word. We cannot help ourselves; one God can give us hope. "But thou hast saved us from our enemies, and hast put them to shame that hated us" (Ps. 44:7, KJV). By keeping our minds focused on God. Our vision will be clear, and we will not walk in darkness. "Let mount Zion rejoice, let the daughters of Judah be glad, because of thy judgments" (Ps. 48:11, KJV). God said he would bring justice, and His people would get the respect they deserve. "So shall the king greatly desire thy beauty: for he is thy Lord; and worship thou him" (Ps. 45:11, KJV). It is very clear who God wants us to worship. He is our hope and strength. "The Lord of hosts is with us; the God of Jacob is our refuge. Selah" (Ps. 46:11, KJV). Our daily walk with the Lord will give us strength and protect us from our enemies in times of trouble.

"Their inward thought is, that their houses shall continue for ever … to all generations; they call their lands after their own names" (Ps. 49:11, KJV). By serving God, there is neither rich nor poor; our investment will be eternal life if we are wise. "I know all the fowls of the mountains: and the wild beasts of the field are mine" (Ps. 50:11, KJV). God knows each one of us by name; He created us, and we can see the beauty of His creation. "Cast me not away from thy presence; and take not thy holy spirit from me" (Ps. 51:11, KJV). We can trust God and ask Him to create a new heart that gives us the strength we need to let the Holy Spirit in. "Wickedness is in the midst thereof: deceit and guide depart not from her streets" (Ps. 55:11, KJV). If we confess our sins, He is faithful to forgive us. There is so much sin out there, and we have to stay close to the Lord avoid temptation .

> **"**
> If we confess our sins, He is faithful to forgive us. There is so much sin out there, and we have to stay close to the Lord avoid temptation.
> **"**

"In God have I put my trust: I will not be afraid what man can do unto me" (Ps. 56:11, KJV). "… We ought to obey God rather than men" (Acts 5:29, KJV). He can take care of all our problems. "Be thou exalted, O God above the heavens; let thy glory be above all the earth" (Ps. 57:5, KJV). We pray for help and God is faithful, with his promises. "So that a man shall say, Verily there is a reward for the righteous: verily he is God that judgeth in the earth" (Ps. 58:11, KJV). There are the just and the unjust people; the just shall rejoin, and the unjust will be judged fairly. "Slay them not, lest my people forget … and bring them down, O Lord our shield" (Ps. 59:11, KJV). His words give us things to look for. That's how much he loves His people. "Give us help from trouble: for vain is the help of man"

(Ps. 60:11, KJV). Our mercies and help come only through God. "God has spoken once; twice have I heard this; that power belongeth unto God" (Ps. 62:11, KJV). Be faithful to God and do the work He asked us to do. Ps. "But the king shall rejoice in God; every one that sweareth by him shall glory: but the mouth of them that speak lies shall be stopped" (Ps. 63:11, KJV). There is a reward for those who swear by the word of God. For those that do not believe, they speak lies. "Thou crownest the year with thy goodness; and thy paths drop fatness" (Ps. 65:11, KJV). Let us praise God and sing for joy. "Thou broughtest us into the net; thou laidst affliction upon our loins" (Ps. 66:11, KJV). We must realize that life is a gift, and it should be cherished.

"The Lord gave the word: great was the company of those that published it" (Ps. 68:11, KJV). We should do what we know is right in God's eyes and be witnesses for Him. "I made sackcloth also my garment; and I become a proverb to them" (Ps. 69:11, KJV). We will do well if we spread His word. Especially when we see they are in darkness, the word had not reached them yet. "Saying thy hath forsaken him: persecute and take him; for there is none to deliver him" (Ps. 71:11, KJV). God does not forsake His people; He takes care of our enemies. "Yea, all kings shall fall down before him: all nations shall serve him" (Ps. 72:11, KJV). All who are righteous will serve Him. He will judge all people. "And they say, how doth God know? and is there knowledge in the most High?" (Ps. 73:11, KJV). Someday, the weak people will see they were on the wrong side, and justice will be served. At the end of time, Satan will lose his power. "Why withdrawest thou thy hand, even thy right hand? Pluck it out of thy bosom" (Ps. 74:11, KJV). God sees and knows the wicked people. We should be patient and wait on God. When the time is right, He will deal with them.

"Vow, and pay unto the Lord your God: let all that be round about him bring presents unto him that ought to be feared" (Ps. 76:11, KJV). We should be moving towards God and make commitments to Him. Praise His name for what He has done in our lives. "I will remember the works of the Lord: surely I will remember thy wonders of old" (Ps. 77:11, KJV). We must remember what the Lord has done for us. Ask the Holy Spirit for faith and strength so we can pull through difficult times. "And forgat his works, and his wonders that he had shewed them" (Ps. 78:11, KJV). Sometimes, God works through those who are most faithful to Him. We have to keep asking for the Holy Spirit to help us. "Let the sighing of the prisoner come before thee; according to the greatness of thy power preserve thou those that are appointed to die" (Ps. 79:11, KJV). God always provides what His people need. He knows the just and the unjust.

"She sent out her boughs unto the sea, and her branches unto the river" (Ps. 80:11, KJV). God casts out His branches where they are needed so they can multiply. He will do what it takes to wake us up. Sometimes, because He loves us. The more we do for Him, the more He can bless. "But my people would not hearken to my voice; and Israel would none of me" (Ps. 81:11, KJV). They murmur and are not respectable with themselves. They are going in the wrong direction. "Make their nobles like Oreb, and like Zeeb: yea, all their princes as

Zebah, and as Zalmunna" (Ps. 83:11, KJV). Our answer is turning to God; call on Him for His protection so we do not fall with the unrighteous or the wrong party. "For the Lord God is a sun and shield: the Lord will give grace and glory: no good thing will he withhold from them that walk uprightly" (Ps. 84:11, KJV). The Lord will not hold anything good from us, but we must obey and walk in His footsteps. "Truth shall spring out of the earth; and righteousness shall look down from heaven" (Ps. 85:11, KJV). Serving God is a beautiful thing. Being faithful to Him, and it

> **We should ask God to teach us His ways. Help me to walk in his truth; ask Him to increase your faith.**

will pay off. If we love Him, we will be faithful. "Teach me thy way, O Lord; I will walk in thy truth: unite my heart to fear thy name" (Ps. 86:11, KJV). We should ask God to teach us His ways. Help me to walk in his truth; ask Him to increase your faith.

CHAPTER NINE

"Shall thy lovingkindness be declared in the grave? Or thy faithfulness in destruction?" (Ps. 88:11, KJV). We should go to God with our feelings because He will listen. We don't need to try and carry it all by ourselves. He tells us to ask, and it shall be given to us. "The heavens are thine, the earth also is thine: as for the world and the fulness thereof, thou hast founded them" (Ps. 89:11, KJV). God's power and purity place Him high above nature and everyone else. "Who knoweth the power of thine anger? even according to thy fear, so is thy wrath" (Ps. 90:11, KJV). God knows all of our sins; we cannot hide them. We can go to Him with our sins, and we must be honest because He still loves us. "For he shall give his angels charge over thee, to keep thee in all thy ways" (Ps. 91:11, KJV).

Each believer has one angel to watch over them, but we cannot see them. Their help is important to us. "The Lord knoweth the thoughts of man, that they are vanity" (Ps. 94:11, KJV). "… Ye shall be holy: for I the Lord am holy" (Lev. 19:2, KJV). He takes us as we are; we should not fear His help. Hebrews discusses how we should encourage, not harden our hearts, and reject sin that would lead us away from God. "Let the heavens rejoice, and let the earth be glad; let the sea roar, and the fulness thereof" (Ps. 96:11, KJV). Hopefully, our desire is God's desire. We will love what He loves. "Light is sown for the righteous, and gladness for the upright in heart" (Ps. 97:11, KJV). Our desire should be in the word of God. When we are familiar with God, our faith increases. "My days are like a shadow that declineth; and I am withered like grass" (Ps. 102:11, KJV). When we feel alone, we should seek God's help. Find a good friend or family member that wants to talk about God. There is someone out there that can help. "For as the heaven is high above the earth, so great is his mercy toward them that fear him" (Ps. 103:11, KJV). He is there for each righteous soul; all we have to do is ask for His help. He is never far from us. We cannot feel we are not good enough to go to Him. He loves everyone. "And the waters covered their enemies: there was not one of them left" (Ps. 106:11, KJV).

When God has done the best He could to have them listen and stay on the right side, He does something about it. He takes care of the evil ones. "Because they rebelled against the words of God, and contemned the counsel of the most high" (Ps. 107:11, KJV). No matter how far we have come, He still loves us. We do not have to stay in prison, all we have to do is confess our sins. He tells us to not sin, but our sins are forgiven. What a loving God we serve! "Wilt not thou, O God, who hast cast us off? and wilt not thou, O God, go forth with our host" (Ps. 108:11, KJV). No matter what we have to go through, God is our helper. "Let the extortioner catch all that he hath; and let the strangers spoil his labour" (Ps. 109:11, KJV). We must hate sin, and God will take care of everything else. God said He will judge the evil people, so praise His name. There will be an end to all that when Jesus comes to take His people home. "Ye that fear the Lord, trust in the Lord: he is their helper and their shield" (Ps. 115:11, KJV). If we belong to God, He will protect his people in times of trouble.

We have to trust Him because He is on our side. "They compassed me about; yea, they compassed me about: but in the name of the Lord I will destroy them" (Ps. 118:11, KJV). We can trust God while we are on earth; we should not put our trust in what we own. We should be preparing for eternal life. "Thy word have I hid in mine heart, that I might not sin against thee" (Ps. 119:11, KJV) We should put God's words in our lives. Like learning a parable. Someone needs your help, and you can share the word of God with them. "The Lord hath sworn in truth unto David; he will not turn from it; Of the fruit of thy body will I set upon thy throne" (Ps. 132:11, KJV). God gave His orders, and there were conditions. We should be helping others find the Lord, and we should be an example to others. They could see something in us that they might want. "And brought out Israel from among them; for his mercy endureth for ever" (Ps. 136:11, KJV). Thank God for His love. We can have love, joy, peace, and trust.

"If I say, Surely the darkness shall cover me; even the night shall be light about me" (Ps. 139:11, KJV). God is light, and when we walk with Him, there is no darkness. He will lead and guide us. "Let not an evil speaker be established in the earth: evil shall hunt the violent man to overthrow him" (Ps. 140:11, KJV). God will protect us from the evil ones. He will lead and guide us. "Rid me, and deliver me from the hand of strange children, whose mouth speaketh vanity, and their right hand is a right hand falsehood" (Ps. 144:11, KJV). God has the power to direct our lives because life is short, and we should live for God. Whether it is a friend or family member, if they speak vanity or what is not of God, we can walk away to pray for them. "They shall speak of the glory of thy kingdom, and talk of thy power" (Ps. 145:11, KJV). God is ready to lift us and carry our burdens. He prepares our hearts to receive the Holy Spirit. God is hope. "The Lord taketh pleasure in them that fear him, in those that hope his mercy" (Ps. 147:11, KJV). Sometimes, our gifts glorify God. If we use our skills for Him, then we will be blessed because He enjoys hearing us praising Him.

In the early seventies, I was hospitalized for twenty-three days due to blood pressure problems. They could not understand why the blood pressure level would go so high in half an hour. It was sky high, one seventy-nine over one seventy. As usual, I went to the Lord and talked to Him. My husband and I talked to our neighbor about attending church with them. They kept the Sabbath but were sometimes off in the scripture. The Lord brought to my mind to read Jude. My answer involved false teachers. In verse four, it talks about certain men crept in unawares, ungodly men, and denying the Lord God. " … there would be mockers in the last time, who should walk after their own ungodly lusts" (Jude 1:18, KJV). "Now unto him that is able to keep you from falling, and to present you faultless before the presence of his glory with exceeding joy" (Jude 1:24, KJV). It says there will be false prophets in the last days, and to be aware of them. God leads you to the truth; you do not want anything else. He lets you recognize if it is not the truth.

"Let not your heart be troubled: ye believe in God, believe also in me" (John 14:1, KJV). And if I go and prepare a place for you, I will come again, and receive you unto myself; that where I am, there ye may be also" (John 14:3, KJV). The gift of God is free salvation; all we have to do is accept His gift and confess our sins. The Holy Spirit will help us to get there. In closing my prayer, I hope it will help someone in need of help. I would not change my walk with the Lord for anything; He gives me so much peace. I realized how important it is to serve Him. Instead of giving Him half an hour of my time, I have Him on my mind. He has blessed me in so many ways, and I do not want to lose him as a friend, a Father, and a King of Kings. God bless.

> **"**
> *The gift of God is free salvation; all we have to do is accept His gift and confess our sins.*
> **"**

Adding to the days in the hospital, They over-medicated me. I requested a transfer to UAB in Birmingham. The teacher of the doctors took my case to a heart specialist. Each one would come every two hours and a nurse every half hour. They took me off of all medicine and started slowly the next day. I had to learn how to walk all again. After a week, they discharged me, and I had to go every three days for a month. I am so sensitive to all medicine; it took three months for me to walk properly.

I'll be 93 in April— I am not complaining. I hope the readers can see how the Lord and Holy Spirit have worked in my life, always leading me to God.

"

I hope the readers can see how the Lord and Holy Spirit have worked in my life, always leading me to God.

"

There is a Savior up there who loves us very much; He just wants a little more of our time. He is there to help us carry our heavy burdens, and you will never be sorry you did. He will be the best friend you ever had because you can always trust him.

* 9 7 8 1 4 7 9 6 1 5 5 1 3 *